QBQ!

THE QUESTION BEHIND THE QUESTION®

Ben—
Thanks for believing
in QBQ!

QBQ!

QBQ!

THE QUESTION BEHIND THE QUESTION®

Practicing Personal Accountability
at Work and in Life

JOHN G. MILLER

G. P. Putnam's Sons   New York

While the author has made every effort to provide accurate telephone
numbers and Internet addresses at the time of publication, neither
the publisher nor the author assumes any responsibility for
errors, or for changes that occur after publication.

G. P. Putnam's Sons
Publishers Since 1838
a member of
Penguin Group (USA) Inc.
375 Hudson Street
New York, NY 10014

Library of Congress Cataloging-in-Publication Data

Miller, John G., date.
QBQ! : the question behind the question: practicing personal accountability
at work and in life / John G. Miller.
p.   cm.
Originally published: Denver, CO : Denver Press, © 2001.
"Practicing personal accountability in business and in life."
ISBN 0-399-15233-4
1. Choice (Psychology).   2. Decision making.   3. Problem solving.
4. Responsibility.   I. Title: Question behind the question.   II. Title.
BF611.M55   2004   2004044733
153.8'3—dc22

Printed in the United States of America
7   9   10   8   6

This book is printed on acid-free paper. ∞

Book design by Amy Thornton

Acknowledgments

Many thanks to:

David Levin, my friend, coach, and writing partner. Without his vision, this book would never have happened

Deb Hvass, a skillful professional writer

Jon Valk, the magic behind the jacket design

Amy Thornton, our layout expert

Maureen Garcia, an excellent illustrator (page 44)

•

Special thanks to my most important team— the one at home in Denver:

The kids: Kristin, Tara, Michael, Molly, Charlene, Jazzy, and Tasha, for putting up with Dad and his hectic schedule during this project

My wife, Karen, for gently encouraging me to do this rewrite of my first book, *Personal Accountability*, and most of all for being my best friend

Contents

·Contents·

·Contents·

I saw the angel in the marble
and I chiseled until
I set it free.

—*Michelangelo*

What Ever Happened To . . .

From a billboard towering over the Houston freeway loomed this question:

"What ever happened to personal responsibility?"

I don't know who put it up there, but it sure jumped out at me. For one thing, it seemed so clearly true. What *has* happened to personal responsibility? Why does it seem the only thing people know how to do anymore is point the finger elsewhere, blaming something or someone else for their problems, their actions, their feelings? Some examples:

I was looking for some coffee in a gas station convenience store, but the carafe was empty, so

I said to the person behind the counter, "Pardon me, there's no coffee in the pot." He pointed at a coworker not fifteen feet away and said, "Coffee is *her* department!"

Department? In a roadside gas station the size of my living room?

Another: On a cross-country flight, the flight attendant got on the intercom and said, "Sorry, everyone, but the movie we promised you will not be shown today. Catering put the wrong one on board."

And this: The carryout pizza place had apparently lost our order, so I was pacing back and forth waiting for our pizzas while my hungry family waited in the car. Suddenly, out of the blue, the young man behind the counter said, "Hey, don't blame *me*, my shift just started!"

In one form or another, we often hear, "It's not my fault," "It's not my job," or "It's not my problem." The billboard jumped out at me partly because I agreed with it so much. But the other thing that struck me was that someone would feel strongly enough about personal responsibility to put it up on a billboard in the first place.

I felt strongly about it, too, and that's why I wrote this book.

Who is this book for? Anyone who's ever heard questions like these:

"When is that department going to do its job?"
"Why don't they communicate better?"
"Who dropped the ball?"
"Why do we have to go through all this change?"
"When is someone going to train me?"

These questions seem innocent enough, but they indicate a lack of personal responsibility— I prefer the term "personal accountability"—and go right to the heart of many of the problems we face today.

Conversely, turning our thinking around and asking more personally accountable questions is one of the most powerful and effective things we can do to improve our organizations and our lives.

The Question Behind the Question® (QBQ®) is a tool that's been developed and refined over the years that helps individuals—including me—practice personal accountability by asking better questions.

I've been writing and speaking about this concept since 1995, and the topic resonates as deeply today as it ever has. Nearly every day I hear new success stories of improved pro-ductivity, greater teamwork, reduced stress, healthier relationships, and better customer service.

The benefit people enjoy the most about the QBQ, though, is a personal one: Once they start practicing QBQ thinking, things just seem to go better. People have more fun. Life is simply more satisfying and enjoyable for those who choose the way of personal accountability.

So if you've heard questions like those listed earlier, if you're frustrated by what you see as a lack of responsibility in others—or if you recognize some of that thinking in yourself—this book is for you. Enjoy!

· CHAPTER ONE ·

A Picture of Personal Accountability

It was a beautiful day in downtown Minneapolis when I stopped into a Rock Bottom restaurant for a quick lunch. The place was jammed. I didn't have much time, so I was happy to grab the one stool they had available at the bar. A few minutes after I sat down, a young man carrying a tray full of dirty dishes hurried past me on his way to the kitchen, but noticing me out of the corner of his eye, stopped, came back and said, "Sir, have you been helped?"

"No, I haven't," I said, "but all I really want is a salad and a couple of rolls."

"I can get you that, sir. What would you like to drink?"

"I'll have a Diet Coke, please."

"Oh, I'm sorry, sir, we sell Pepsi. Would that be all right?"

"Ah, no thanks," I said with a smile, "I'll just have water with lemon, please."

"Great, I'll be back." He disappeared.

Moments later he came back with the salad, the rolls, and the water. I thanked him, and he was quickly gone again, leaving me to enjoy my meal, a satisfied customer.

Suddenly, there was a blur of activity off to my left, the "wind of enthusiasm" stirred behind me, and then, over my right shoulder stretched the "long arm of service," delivering a twenty-ounce bottle, frosty on the outside, cold on the inside, of—you guessed it—Diet Coke!

"Wow!" I said. "Thank you!"

"You're welcome," he said with a smile, and hurried off again.

My first thought was "Hire this man!" Talk about going the extra mile! He was clearly not your average employee. But the more I thought about the extraordinary thing he'd just done, the more I wanted to talk to him. So as soon as I could get his attention, I waved him over.

"Excuse me, I thought you didn't sell Coke," I said.

"That's right, sir, we don't."

"Well, where did this come from?"

"The grocery store around the corner, sir."

I was taken aback.

"Who paid for it?" I asked.

"I did, sir; just a dollar."

By then I was thinking profound and professional thoughts like "Cool!" But what I said was, "Come on, you've been awfully busy. How did you have time to go get it?" Smiling and seemingly growing taller before my eyes, he said, "I didn't, sir. *I sent my manager!*"

I couldn't believe it. Was that empowerment

or what? I'll bet we can all think of times we would love to look at our "boss" and say, "Get me a Diet Coke!" What a great image. But beyond that, his actions paint a marvelous picture of personal accountability and The Question Behind the Question. We'll go into the specifics of the QBQ in the chapters to come, but for now let's take a look at my server's thinking and the choices he made.

It was the lunch rush. He was already busy, with plenty to do. But he noticed a customer who, though not in his section, looked as though he needed some attention, so he decided to do what he could to help. I don't know what was in his mind at that moment, of course, but faced with a similar situation, many people would have had thoughts like these:

"Why do I have to do everything around here?"
"Who's supposed to be covering this area, anyway?"

"When is management going to provide us with more products?"

"Why are we always so short-staffed?"

"When are the customers going to learn to read the menu?"

It's understandable that someone would feel and think that way, especially when frustrated, but the truth is that these are lousy questions. They're negative and they don't solve any problems. Throughout the rest of the book we'll refer to questions like these as Incorrect Questions, or IQs, since nothing positive or productive comes from asking them. They're also the complete opposite of personal accountability, because in each one, the implication is that someone or something else is responsible for the problem or situation.

Unfortunately, though, they're often the first thoughts that come to mind. It's a sad fact that when most of us are faced with a frustration or challenge of some kind, our first reaction tends to be negative and defensive, and the first questions that occur to us are IQs.

The good news is this: That moment of frustration also presents us with a tremendous opportunity to contribute, and the QBQ can help us take advantage of it. The moment the IQs pop into our heads, we have a choice. We can either accept them—"Yeah, when *are* we going to get more help around here?!"—or reject them, choosing instead to ask better, more accountable questions such as "What can *I* do to make a difference?" and "How can *I* support the team?"

This, in a nutshell, is the essence of the QBQ:

Making better choices in the moment by asking better questions.

That's exactly what my server did. He didn't ask IQs and get caught in the downside of the situation. Instead—in the moment—he disciplined his thoughts, made better choices and asked better questions. Whether he used the words or not, his actions clearly indicated accountable thinking such as "What can I do to help out?" and "How can I provide value to you?" His choices made the difference.

As I left that day, I gave him a good tip, as anyone would have, bouncing my quarters across the bar. (Just kidding. It was the excellent tip he deserved.) And when I returned a couple of months later and asked for "my favorite server, Jacob Miller"—I love his last name— the hostess said, "I'm sorry, sir, Jacob is no longer . . ."

My thoughts flew fast. "NO! You lost my own personal server? You lost a guy who looked at me and thought, 'What can I do right now to serve you?'!" I just couldn't believe they had let him get away.

But I didn't say any of that to her. I simply interrupted with, "Oh no, you lost him?" to which she brightly responded, "Oh, no sir, we didn't lose him, he was promoted to management."

My first thought was *"Management*, what a waste!"* (Go ahead, smile—even if you're a manager.)

The truth is, I wasn't at all surprised that Jacob, with the way he thought, would be so quickly on his way toward his chosen goals. That's the difference personal accountability can make. Everyone wins: customers, coworkers, the organization, everyone. And for Jacob, beyond the tips and the promotion, I can't help but think the greatest win of all is the way he must feel about himself at the end of a day of making better choices, asking better questions, and practicing personal accountability.

CHAPTER TWO

Making Better Choices

Soon after we moved to Denver, we discovered something we'd never seen before: goat heads. Goat heads are wicked little thorns that grow in this part of the country and have what look like the ears, horns, and nose of a goat. They fall to the ground with their horns pointing in the air, and if one happens to work its way into your shoe—or your bike tire—it can really ruin your day.

In fact, if you live in the West, it will come as no surprise to you that we've changed more bicycle tires since moving here than during all the years that we lived in the Upper Midwest combined. Serious bikers take multiple precautions against goat heads for even the thickest mountain bike tires.

Each day, as we journey into the unexplored wilds of our personal and professional lives, we have countless choices to make. And what are we choosing? Not our next action but our next thought. Choose the wrong thought and we're off in the emotional goat heads of blame, complaining, and procrastination. But the right thoughts lead us to a richer, more fulfilling life and the feelings of pride and accomplishment that come from making productive decisions.

The idea that we are accountable for our own choices and are free to make better ones is fundamental to the QBQ. Sometimes people think they have no choice. They'll say things like "I have to" or "I can't." But we always have a choice. Always. Even deciding *not* to choose is making a choice. Realizing this and taking responsibility

for our choices is a big step toward making great
things happen in our lives.

Want to avoid the goat heads and make great
things happen?

Make better choices.

CHAPTER THREE

QBQ! The Question Behind the Question

Now let's talk about the tool that brings personal accountability to life: the QBQ.

The Question Behind the Question is built on the observation that our first reactions are often negative, bringing to mind Incorrect Questions (IQs). But if in each moment of decision we can instead discipline our thoughts to look behind those initial questions and ask better ones (QBQs), the questions themselves will lead us to better results.

One of the guiding principles of the QBQ is

"The answers are in the questions," which speaks to the same truth: If we ask a better question, we get a better answer. So the QBQ is about asking better questions. But how can we tell a good question from a bad one? What does a "better" question sound like?

This book will help each of us learn to recognize and ask better questions. For starters, here are the three simple guidelines for creating a QBQ:

1. Begin with "What" or "How" (**not** "Why," "When," or "Who").
2. Contain an "I" (**not** "they," "them," "we," or "you").
3. Focus on action.

"What can I do?" for example, follows the guidelines perfectly. It begins with "What," contains an "I," and focuses on action: "What can

I do?" Simple, as I said. But don't let its
simplicity fool you. Like a jewel, the QBQ is made
up of many facets. In the following chapters,
we'll explore these facets and see the powerful
effect asking QBQs can have on our lives.

CHAPTER FOUR

Don't Ask "Why?"

Ever heard these questions?

"Why don't others work harder?"
"Why is this happening to me?"
"Why do they make it so difficult for me to do
my job?"

Say them aloud. How do they make you feel? When I say them, I feel powerless, like a victim. Questions with a "Why me?" tone to them say, "I'm a victim of the environment and the people around me." Not a very productive thought, is it? But we ask them all the time.

(Quick point: If you've been trained on the

"Five Whys" of problem solving or selling, that's not what we're talking about here. Those are useful and appropriate. What we're referring to are questions that begin with "Why" and have the "poor me" tone that leads straight to the classic pity party.)

Anyone can fall into the "Why" trap. I asked a department manager once how many people worked for him, and he said, "About half!" It's a funny line, but he was undoubtedly the kind of manager who would also ask the IQs, "Why can't I find good people?" "Why doesn't the younger generation really want to work?" "Why don't I get more direction from upper management?"

That's all victim thinking, and there's too much of it in the world already.

I was on a long flight, sitting next to a man in his mid-fifties. We introduced ourselves and started a friendly conversation along the lines of "Where are you heading?" and "What do you do?" It turns out he owns a second home near

Aspen and was just returning from a twenty-one-day ski vacation. "Wow!" I thought. "Twenty-one days in Aspen. This man has some discretionary income!" He went on to say that he lives in New York City and works on Wall Street. Guess what he does? He's not a broker. He's a personal injury attorney.

When he asked me what I do, I opted for the quick, easy answer, "Author, speaker." "Oh, really?" he said. "What do you speak about?" I considered this for a moment and thought, "Why not?" So I said what I always say, "Personal accountability," wondering if he'd see the irony—and the humor. It took a couple of moments. We stared at each other. He fidgeted a bit. Finally, just to be clear, I added, "What I really do is help people—including myself—eliminate *victim thinking* from their lives." He must have understood me then because he got up and moved and we never spoke again!

I have nothing against him or his profession.

He's simply providing what's demanded by a culture that continually asks, "Why is this happening to me?" But even as we shake our heads about the ills of society, let's not forget that society is made up of individuals. You and me. The best thing we can do to get rid of victim thinking in our world is to get rid of it in ourselves.

The first QBQ guideline says all QBQs begin with "What" or "How," not "Why," "When," or "Who." Take another look at the "Why" questions at the beginning of the chapter and consider what would happen if we asked these instead:

"How can I do my job better today?"
"What can I do to improve the situation?"
"How can I support others?"

CHAPTER FIVE

The Victim

I received an e-mail from a gentleman who wrote that during his ten years in the military, whenever something went wrong, the only acceptable response was "No excuses, sir!" He accepted it, he believed it, and he lived it.

When he returned to civilian life, he started working as a territory manager for a large firm in the food industry. He wasn't doing as well as his company expected, and he wasn't pleased with his own performance, either. The day before he went through an in-house training program on personal accountability and the QBQ, he had gone to his manager and asked questions like these:

"Why don't you give me more of your time?"
"Why don't you coach me more?"
"Why aren't we more competitive?"
"Why don't we get some new products?"
"Why doesn't marketing support us more?"

He closed his e-mail saying, "I realized when I learned the QBQ that from military to business, in just a few short years, I had become what I hated the most: *the victim*." If this man, after ten years of living and breathing "No excuses!" can slip into victim thinking, it's no wonder the rest of us have to be on the lookout for it in our own lives.

CHAPTER SIX

"Why Is This Happening to Me?"

Stress is a choice. Do you buy that? Some people have a hard time with the idea. They think it's the people and events in our lives that stress us out—management, colleagues, customers, the boss, traffic, weather, market conditions—but it isn't true.

Yes, bad things happen: The economy sours, our business struggles, the stock market tumbles, jobs are lost, people around us don't follow through, deadlines are missed, projects fail, good people leave. Life is full of these. But still, stress is a choice, because whatever the "trigger event," we always choose our own response. We choose to react angrily. We choose to stuff our emotions and keep quiet. We choose to worry. (One client had a sign on his desk that said "I've had many problems, some of which came true!") Different people have different reactions to the same situation. Stress is a choice.

Stress is also the *result* of our choices. When we choose to ask a question like "Why is this happening to me?" we feel as if we have no control. This leads us to a victim mindset, which is extremely stressful. Even in cases where we actually *are* victims and our feelings seem justified, "Why me?" thinking only adds to our stress.

CHAPTER SEVEN

"Why Do We Have to Go Through All This Change?"

When Stacey was twelve years old, she and her father, a pilot, took off on a Sunday afternoon joy-ride in their single-engine Cessna. Not long into the flight, and about a mile up over Lake Michigan, the joy of their father-daughter adventure came to an abrupt halt. The engine quit.

Stacey's father turned to her and in a calm, reassuring tone said, "Honey, the engine has quit. I'm going to need to fly the plane differently." Interesting phrase: "Fly the plane differently."

Her father understood that new challenges

and changing conditions often require different strategies. Conditions change, markets change, people change. What works one day in a given situation does not necessarily work the next. We need to develop a repertoire of responses so we're prepared when our engine unexpectedly quits.

In order to restart the engine, they needed more air speed. Stacey's father told her he would be hitting switches in the cockpit while he steered the plane downward. ("Toward the deep, cold waters of Lake Michigan!" I thought as she told me the story.) Stacey understood, and sensing the gravity of the situation, quickly nodded her approval of Dad's plan. (This did not go off to the headquarters for a committee decision— a term that always strikes me as an oxymoron.)

Her father put the plane into a dive and fiddled with the switches, but nothing happened. He leveled off closer to the water. "Stacey, we're going to try that again," he said. "Hang on!" They dove a second time. He hit the switches again as the plane gained speed, and this time the engine fired, first with just a few hopeful sputters, but finally with a secure, familiar hum.

About twenty minutes later, they landed safely. At that point, this Rock of Gibraltar kind of guy, this Fearless Father, this Man of Courage turned to his twelve-year-old daughter, lovingly patted her shoulder, and said, "Now honey, whatever you do, *don't tell Mom!*"

I love this story. Not just for the drama and the humor, but for what it says about handling change. When faced with a new situation, Stacey's dad took action and solved the problem. But if he had resisted the change and instead spent his time whining and complaining, having thoughts like "Well, I've never done it that way before!" or asking IQs such as "Why do we have to go through all this change?" things might have turned out much differently.

Are you facing change? Any engines quit in your life lately? If so, ask a better question. Here's one that really works: "How can I *adapt* to the changing world?"

CHAPTER EIGHT

"Why Don't They Communicate Better?"

In the many workshops I've facilitated over the years, this scene has played out over and over again: I'll ask, "What's the critical issue facing your organization today?" Generally, the answer is not change or competition, but communication. Then it's framed like this: "Why don't they communicate better?"

Actually, communication means not only being understood but also understanding the other person. The QBQ is "How can I better understand you?"

Understand?

CHAPTER NINE

Don't Ask "When?"

"When will they take care of the problem?"
"When will the customer call me back?"
"When will we get the information we need
   to make a decision?"

When we ask "When?" we're really saying we
have no choice but to wait and put off action until
another time. Questions that begin with "When"
lead to procrastination.

I don't believe most people intend to procrastinate. Certainly no one ever gets out of bed and
says, "Today, I'm going to procrastinate!" (Even a
hard-core procrastinator who might want to say
all that would put it off until tomorrow.) But

procrastination is a sneaky problem. We put something off until a little later, and then a little later, and a little later again until, before we know it, the action has been postponed so long that it has become a serious problem.

Is any procrastination going on in your life? Most people don't hesitate to admit that procrastination is a problem for them. And if it's a problem for most people, it's also a problem for most organizations. What are the consequences? Putting things off means precious time is lost. Productivity suffers. The team may not progress toward its goal. Deadlines are missed.

As a client once said, "Long-range vision and strategic planning are great tools, but we need to get some things done before lunch!"

Procrastination also increases stress. As things pile up, we begin to feel overwhelmed, which takes the joy out of our work. Bottom line: Procrastination is costly to all involved.

Why do we do it? I'm sure there are reasons

we could explore, but frankly, I'd prefer to talk about solutions. And one solution is to stop asking externally focused questions that begin with "When?" Instead, we need to ask QBQs such as:

"What solution can I provide?"
"How can I more creatively reach the customer?"
"What can I do to find the information to make a decision?"

Remember: The answers are in the questions.

· CHAPTER TEN ·

Procrastination: The Friend of Failure

I decided to give away a very large, old wooden desk, topped with a piece of quarter-inch-thick clear glass, about three feet by five feet. The new owner didn't want the glass. When we loaded the desk into his truck early one Saturday morning, we left the sheet of glass leaning against the basketball hoop pole at the edge of our driveway.

As my friend drove away with the desk, he said, "You'd better put that glass in a safe place." I yelled back, "I will!" But I didn't. I glanced at it and told myself I'd do it later. Then I got busy trimming bushes and cleaning the garage. Every time I walked by that sheet of glass, I told myself that I should move it before it blew over. "I'll do it later," I kept thinking.

The day wore on, and we decided to go out to dinner as a family. As we backed out of the driveway, my wife, Karen, said, "Shouldn't we put that glass someplace safe?" You know what I told her.

A couple of hours later, we arrived home at dusk, and were all heading into the house when I spotted a small pair of grass clippers sitting near the curb under a streetlight. I said to our son, Michael, who was nine, "Mike, would you go over there and grab those clippers and put them in the garage for me, please?" Off he went as I headed into the house.

It was a quiet Saturday evening in our pleasant neighborhood, until the silence was broken by the most terrifying sound I have ever heard: the shattering of a large piece of plate glass.

I realized instantly what had happened. I also knew why. I dashed out of the garage and around our car to find Michael lying in the driveway on his stomach atop hundreds of deadly shards of glass, some more than a foot long. He was crying as I ran, carrying him, to the front porch. I held him under the light to check his injuries, expecting the worst, and I couldn't believe what I saw: not a scratch! He had run right into the glass and fallen on top of it as it hit the pavement, but there wasn't a mark on him. To say we felt incredibly thankful would be an understatement.

Why did this incident happen? Procrastination, the Friend of Failure. I knew the glass needed to be put away, and doing so would have taken no more than a few minutes. But I put it off and put it off, until finally it exploded into what could have been a catastrophe.

Let's take care of the little things while they're still little.

CHAPTER ELEVEN

"When Will We Get More Tools and Better Systems?"

Most of us have heard the saying "Creativity is thinking outside the box." There's a lot of truth in that, but to me true creativity is this:

Succeeding *within* the box.

Hitting targets, reaching goals, doing the job well, and making a difference with what we already have is the QBQ way. Every organization has imperfect systems and finite resources. We may wish we had newer tools, better systems, more people, and bigger budgets. But thinking too much about what we'd like to have is another cause of procrastination. Managers, for example, won't take their group through team-building until "all the right people are in place." Individuals won't make a decision until they have all the information, or take action until all the questions are answered.

Ironically, succeeding with what we have makes us more likely to get the things we wanted in the first place. Listen to the wisdom of Deb Weber of State Farm Insurance: "I find that every time I do the job with the tools I have, I tend to receive more tools." It's a truth: We sow, then we reap.

Focusing on what we don't have is a waste of time and energy. To really make a difference, let's instead focus our energy on succeeding within the box. Let's ask the QBQ "How can I achieve with the resources I already have?"

CHAPTER TWELVE

"When Are We Going to Hear Something New?"

Sales can be a difficult profession, but it is not complicated. If salespeople consistently practice the fundamentals—getting up early, contacting prospective clients, sharing their belief in the value of their products and services, following up—they'll be successful.

But I can't tell you how many times salespeople have come up and asked something like, "John, I've taken Selling Skills 101. What's next?" My answer? "NOTHING!" The problem is not a shortage of new ideas but a lack of understanding that the "old" ideas still work.

This may not be true with technology, which changes every five minutes, but when it comes to the principles on which we can base our organizations and lives, the *old* stuff is the *good* stuff.

How often in our organizations have we brought in the "blue" program, the "red" program, and the "green" program—all inside of ninety days—only to have them make little difference anyway because there are no quick fixes for long-term problems? We don't need the "new" thing or the "hot" topic. What we need to do is practice the fundamentals—like personal accountability—day in and day out.

"When are we going to hear something new?" is the wrong question. The right one is "How can I *apply* what I'm hearing?"—even if I've heard it before.

Chapter Thirteen

Don't Ask "Who?"

"Who made the mistake?"
"Who missed the deadline?"
"Who dropped the ball?"

When we ask "Who" questions like these, what we're really doing is looking for scapegoats, someone else to blame. And blame may well be the most pervasive and counterproductive of all the ideas we've talked about so far. Flip forward to the image on page 44: arms crossed, fingers pointed at everyone else. I call this the "Company Coat of Arms." If organizations had separate logos to represent their internal identities, too often this would be it.

The Company Coat of Arms

While riding in a van from Snowbird Ski Resort in Utah to the Salt Lake City airport, I struck up a conversation with the driver. Turned out he doubled as the sales manager for the transportation firm. As we talked about the subject of blame, he said, "Oh, we've got lots of blame going on in our company!"

"Really?" I said.

"Yeah," he continued. "The receptionist blames the dispatchers, who blame the drivers, who blame the salespeople, who blame me . . ."

I stopped him. "How many people are in your firm?"

"Twelve," he said. Twelve people! I guess you don't have to be big to play the blame game.

From the smallest group to the largest corporation, from the lowest rung on the ladder to the highest office in the land, there's an epidemic of blame going on, and no one seems immune. The CEO blames the vice president, who blames the manager, who blames the employee, who blames the customer, who blames the government, who blames the people, who blame the politicians, who blame the schools, who blame the parents, who blame the teen, who blames the dad, who blames the mom, who blames her manager, who blames the vice president, who blames the CEO, and on and on it goes. This is the "Circle of Blame," and it would be kind of funny if it weren't so true.

Blame and "whodunit" questions solve nothing. They create fear, destroy creativity, and build walls. Instead of brainstorming and working together to get things done, we *blame*-storm and accomplish nothing. There's not a chance we'll reach our full potential until we stop blaming each other and start practicing personal accountability.

"What can I do today to solve the problem?"
"How can I help move the project
    forward?"

"What action can I take to 'own' the situation?"

Try these questions instead of the "Who?" questions at the beginning of this chapter and see how fast you can break the Circle of Blame in your organization.

CHAPTER FOURTEEN

A Poor Sailor
Blames the Wind

Have you ever heard the saying "A poor sailor blames the wind"? How about "A poor worker blames the tool" or "A poor coach blames the players"? Let's have some fun and carry this idea further:

A poor teacher blames the _____.

A poor salesperson blames the _____.

A poor parent blames the _____.

A poor manager blames the _____.

· A Poor Sailor Blames the Wind ·

A poor employee blames the _____.

A poor coach blames the _____.

A poor teenager blames the—world!

Whom do accountable people blame? No one. Not even themselves.

CHAPTER FIFTEEN

Silos

"You're kidding!" I said. "You don't have a 'we/they' syndrome here?" Kevin, a vice president of operations, sat smiling and shaking his head as I continued. "No cross-functional friction? No field-versus-corporate mentality? No management-versus-employees attitude? No 'we/they'?!" I couldn't believe it. If it were true, his would be the first organization I'd ever seen that didn't have this problem.

"Nope," he said and added with a smirk, "There's no 'we/they' here. But it is *'us against them!'*"

Kevin was having a little fun. "Of course," his

joke implied, "of course we have a 'we/they' syndrome. Who doesn't?"

I met another executive who had a more direct way of putting it: "John, I can sum up all our problems in a few words: 'silos and butt-covering.'"

Do you have silos in your organization, called accounting, sales, manufacturing, marketing, R&D, operations, administration, the home office, or the field? Can people be heard claiming in some way, "That's not my job," while the walls grow taller, stronger, and more difficult to over-come? I know of one company whose field sales organization actually refers to its own head-quarters as the "Sales Prevention Club"! Then there was the customer service person at a specialty catalog house (I'd called in to check on an overdue order) who told me, "Yeah, the ship-ping department is doing it to us again!" Us? Whose team does she think she's on?

For all the time and resources our organizations spend on team-building, we still seem to forget one simple truth: We're all on the *same* team. Every day, we see groups, departments, regions, and individuals work at cross purposes. Our so-called teams bicker and complain about the "others" who don't "do their jobs right." This kind of compartmentalization and infighting drains the life right out of an organization. It's like having a tandem bike with the riders facing in opposite directions: lots of activity, lots of exertion, but no forward movement.

With competitors working to beat us every day, can we really afford to be working against each other, too? Let's climb out of our silos, forget the "we/they," and remember: We're all on the same team.

· CHAPTER SIXTEEN ·

Beat the Ref

My father, Jimmy Miller, was head wrestling coach at Cornell University in Ithaca, New York, for more than twenty-five years. When he sent me out to the mat, he'd always remind me I had three people to beat that day: my opponent, myself, and the referee.

That I had to beat my opponent was obvious. By "myself" he meant I had to overcome the fears any athlete naturally has. About beating the ref, he'd say, "It doesn't matter how close the match is, John. Even if you lose in overtime by one point, even if he makes a couple of questionable calls, you cannot blame the man in black and

· 53 ·

white." He'd conclude by saying, "If you want to win, you must be good enough to beat the ref!"

Good enough to beat the ref. That means being a salesperson who has the maturity to say, "I was outsold," instead of complaining about the product, the price, and the lack of advertising. It means serving as a team member who never says, "Why don't others pull their own weight?" It means being a manager who doesn't complain, "Why aren't my people motivated?" It means being the people who don't complain about management, saying, "Why don't they tell us what's going on?"

Who is the "ref" in your life? What person or situation beyond your control is standing between you and success? Could it be a supervisor who over-manages, making it difficult for you to do your job, or inefficient systems built into your organization that waste a lot of your time? Or maybe it's a personal situation that saps your energy.

No matter what we're trying to accomplish, there's always a barrier of some kind to overcome, and it's often something over which we have no control. Instead of focusing on the barriers, let's work to become so good that we'll succeed no matter how many bad calls the ref may throw at us.

If you want to win, don't complain about things beyond your control. Just be good enough to beat the ref.

CHAPTER SEVENTEEN

"Who Dropped the Ball?"

It was a humid day in Houston. As I boarded the plane, I could feel the heat in the steamy, crowded cabin. The flight was obviously over-booked, and every passenger seemed to have three pieces of large carry-on luggage. On top of that, several people had apparently been assigned the same seats and weren't taking it well. Tension in the cabin was high.

The doors finally closed, and we taxied to the runway, only to sit for another full hour, with no explanation from the crew. I couldn't help but think this gave a whole new meaning to the term "pressurized cabin." Mercifully, we did finally take off, and that's when I met one of my QBQ heroes.

Bonita was a flight attendant. When I first saw her, she was prancing down the aisle with an armload of headphones, smiling broadly and having great fun. It was the week before Christmas, and she was wearing one of those red-and-white Santa Claus caps, which draped down her shoulder and off to one side.

As she handed out the headphones, she wasn't saying, "We held you up for an hour, but give me five bucks anyway!" She was offering them at no charge. I watched her turn to a young man and say, "I'm sure you'll enjoy our sports programming, sir. Here are some headphones!" And to a woman, "I notice you're traveling alone, ma'am, would you like a friend?"

When she got to me, I stopped her and said, "You know, Bonita, I really appreciate your attitude!" As she sashayed away with that big smile on her face and the Santa Claus cap on her head, she said, "Well, whatever you do, don't drug test me!"

I didn't need to test her. I already knew she was high—on life. And that's one of the great things that happens when we make better choices: We get high on life.

It's not about "us" versus "them" or "Why did they overbook the plane?" or "Who dropped the ball?" The better question is "What can I do right now to make a difference?"

With one simple choice, making the best of a bad situation, Bonita made a difference for me and every other person on that flight. That's how personal accountability changes the world: one choice at a time.

CHAPTER EIGHTEEN

Ownership

People frequently talk about a need for "ownership" in our organizations. This story illustrates what they mean:

I was having a problem with static in my phone line, so I contacted our phone company to request a service call. A repairman showed up, worked hard on the line, and left. But the static came back the next day. A second repairman came and worked on it some more, but the problem returned. When the third guy came, I described the problem, paused, and waited for the blame to roll. I fully expected him to bad-mouth his associates, but he didn't. Instead, he said something very powerful: "Mr. Miller, I can't explain it, but I sure can apologize for it!"

Ownership: "A commitment of the head, heart, and hands to *fix* the problem and never again *affix* the blame."

Have you made that commitment?

· CHAPTER NINETEEN ·

The Foundation of Teamwork

Would you watch a bald eagle soar and say, "I wish he could swim the seas like a dolphin?" Would you look at a dolphin and hope it someday might reach the heavens like a giraffe? Would you think, "Why can't the lion run as fast as the cheetah?" No, of course not. How ridiculous.

Are you on teams with people who are different from you?

"A teammate is someone who can look right through you and still enjoy the view." Let's appreciate people's gifts and strengths just as they are. That's the foundation of teamwork.

CHAPTER TWENTY

Making Accountability Personal: All QBQs Contain an "I"

Right after I had spoken on personal account-ability and the QBQ, the CEO of the company I was addressing got up to say a few words. After a few comments to the hundreds of people before him, he pressed a button that projected this mes-sage on a huge screen behind him:

"Personal accountability begins with YOU!"

I know what he was trying to say, but he missed the mark. Personal accountability does NOT begin with you. It begins with me. That's why it's called *personal* accountability. It is not about you or me holding each other accountable, as a manager does in setting standards, defining consequences, helping set goals, and then holding people accountable for their performance. Nor is it a group thing, where people get together, make public professions of commitment, then come back a week or a month later to discuss what did or did not happen.

Personal accountability is about each of us holding *ourselves* accountable for our own thinking and behaviors and the results they produce.

This is why the second QBQ guideline is: All QBQs contain an "I," **not** "they," "them," "we," or "you." Questions that contain an "I" turn our focus away from other people and circumstances and put it back on ourselves, where it can do the most good. We can't change other people. We often can't control circumstances and events. The only things we have any real control over are our own thoughts and actions. Asking questions that focus our efforts and energy on what we can do makes us significantly more effective, not to mention happier and less frustrated.

Accountability groups are great tools. Managers and executives *do* need to define and communicate standards, but the power of personal accountability comes from questions that begin with "What" or "How" and contain an "I."

CHAPTER TWENTY-ONE

I Can Only Change Me

Who is the only person I can change? Right—myself. I bet you've known that for a long time. So basic. So fundamental. Here's another question for you: As you've been reading this material, who have you been picturing, thinking, "I wish they could hear this, because they need it?!" It happens all the time. We say, "I can only change me," but then when asked, "Who have you been thinking needs the QBQ?" we say "They do!"

Have you tried to "fix" anybody lately? We all do it. Some of us don't think we're trying to change people, even when we are. A director of a nonprofit said to his four team members in a roundtable discussion, "Really, I'm not trying to change my assistant. I'm not! I just think she should set more long-term goals for herself." Translation: "I want her to be what *I* want her to be."

Others know they're doing it but don't want to admit it. I was talking with a training manager, making final arrangements for delivering a QBQ program for her organization. She said, "Do you want to know why the VP is investing in this program?"

"Sure," I said, cautiously, wondering where this was leading.

"He wants to fix Ed."

Fix Ed?

Ed, she went on to explain, was a supervisor

who was struggling in his role. But instead of taking responsibility and dealing with the situation in a direct and honest way, the VP was going to put the whole team through training. "Fix Ed." Those words have always stuck in my mind.

Still others think it's their job to change people. I was visiting with a man in his late twenties who actually said, "I believe it's my job to change people—I'm a manager!" Sorry. Managers don't change people. They can coach, counsel, teach, and guide, but no one changes another person. Change *only* comes from the inside, as a result of decisions made by the individual.

This is a hard lesson to learn, and even when we say we "get it," there's a big difference between understanding the idea "Yes, I can only change myself!" and honestly examining the reality of our thoughts and actions.

Frequently I'll ask a group, "What's the *one* thing you would change to improve the effectiveness of your organization?" Usually they come out with a list of "Ps": Products, Promotions, **Policies**, **Processes**, Procedures, Pricing, and **People**. More people, fewer people, different people. One guy said, "Pepsi." (Yes, Pepsi.) "If only we'd switch the pop machine in the break room from Coke to Pepsi."

People's minds fill with all kinds of ideas when asked what they would change to improve things. But guess what? Nobody ever says "Me!" "I would change *me* to make our organization run more effectively." Someone once suggested it was a trick question, but I don't think it is. Read it again. Our minds simply don't go there. Our thoughts almost always focus elsewhere first. Asking questions that begin with "What" or "How" and contain an "I" brings our focus back to ourselves.

How much better things would be if we all tried to mold and shape our own thoughts and actions rather than those of others. The bottom line is that the QBQ works because it's based on the truth *"I can only change me."*

Chapter Twenty-two

"He Didn't, I Did"

After a presentation, a middle manager at Jostens (the class ring and yearbook company) came up and told me that the idea "I can only change me" had really touched her. "When I was a branch manager," she explained, "there was a guy reporting to me who I just couldn't seem to manage. We didn't work well together at all. When he transferred to another location across the country, I was relieved.

"A couple of years went by. We found ourselves in the same office, and I was his supervisor again. But this time things were different," she said. "We were getting along, communicating well, and cooperating on projects. At one point I asked myself, 'When did he change?' but then I realized he hadn't changed, I had!"

"How had you changed?" I asked. Her response nailed it right on the head:

"I stopped trying to change him."

CHAPTER TWENTY-THREE.

"When Will Others Walk Their Talk?"

Up to the mountaintop go the executives for a senior management retreat. For three days they debate the critical issues, filling flip charts with brightly colored ink. Finally, "mission, vision, and values" in hand, they return to the valley below where the people wait to receive the stone tablets, which have been magically transformed into little laminated pocket cards for men to sit on and women to stuff in their briefcases.

Not long after, people huddle near a water cooler, pull out their cards, and whisper, "Well, I'll practice these values when *they* do!"

Careful. The easiest thing to spot is gaps of integrity in others:

The manager who says, "I'm here to help you reach your personal goals," and then dresses people down in front of others.

The executive who says, "You are all empowered. It's our new program!" and then adds, "But before you do anything substantial, check with me first."

The teammate who says, "I appreciate my colleagues just the way they are . . . but if they'd only be a bit more like me."

The organization that proudly declares on the lobby wall its guiding value, "People are our greatest asset!" yet the training dollar is the last one budgeted and the first one cut.

The definition of integrity is this:

"Being what I say I am by acting in accordance with my words."

QBQ thinking leads to integrity because integrity begins with me—not others—asking the question "How can I practice the principles I espouse?"

Instead of asking "When will others walk their talk?" let's walk our own talk first.

CHAPTER TWENTY-FOUR

An Integrity Test

Here's an integrity test for anyone who's part of an organization: Does what we say about our organization while we're at work *match* what we say at home? If it's positive at work and negative a few hours later at home, we have a choice to make. Here's an idea we should all consider:

Believe or leave.

Sound harsh? Maybe. But if the organization is no longer a vehicle to help us reach our life goals, why would we stay?

Answering that question honestly is part of practicing personal accountability.

CHAPTER TWENTY-FIVE

The Power of One

One of the most tempting questions to ask when we first learn the QBQ is "What can *we* do?" The problem is "we" don't change. Teams, departments, and organizations don't change. People change, one at a time, through their own choices.

I'm a firm believer in the team concept, but if we're not careful, we can end up substituting the language of teams ("we" and "us") for the language of personal accountability. We can hide behind the team with thoughts—which become excuses—such as:

"The team didn't meet the deadline."
"The team wasn't given enough resources."

"The team didn't get the job done."

"The team didn't have a clear mission."

Personal accountability is not about changing others. It's about making a difference by changing ourselves.

Personal accountability. The power of one.

CHAPTER TWENTY-SIX

A QBQ Twist

You may already be familiar with the Serenity Prayer:

"God grant me the serenity to accept the things I cannot change, the courage to change the things I can, and the wisdom to know the difference."

Here's a QBQ twist for all of us:

"God grant me the serenity to accept the people I cannot change, the courage to change the one I can, and the wisdom to know ... *it's me!*"

CHAPTER TWENTY-SEVEN.

Will the Real Role Models Please Stand Up!

We make a tremendous fuss when a Hollywood star, sports figure, pop singer, or politician gets out of line. "Shame on them," we say, for being such a bad role model for the children. But in reality, no public figure is a role model for our kids. That's our job—yours and mine. It's a humbling realization at times, but it's the truth.

It's equally true for all of us. No matter what our role, someone is watching and emulating our behavior.

Modeling is the most powerful of all teachers.

Who's watching you?

Chapter Twenty-eight

Practicing Personal Accountability: All QBQs Focus on Action

A corporation that had just gone through a major merger held a QBQ session. Afterward, a middle manager came up and shared this story with me. He had come into our morning program griping and complaining (his words) about a problem with the new parent company head-quarters in New Jersey, which was seriously hampering his field operations. After an hour or so of the QBQ, he began to think differently. He slipped out and called his travel agent to book a ticket for the next day back to the East Coast. He had figured out how to solve the problem.

What a great example of the practice of personal accountability. First, he chose to stop complaining and ask a better question like "What can I do?" And when the better answer came— "You know what? I could head out there, sit down with them, and figure this thing out"—he did it. He picked up the phone and made the call.

It's so simple, but the ultimate goal of the QBQ is action!

Our third guideline is: All QBQs focus on action. To make a QBQ action-focused, we add verbs such as "do," "make," "achieve," and "build" to questions that start with "What" or "How" and contain an "I."

Now, if that's all we did, a QBQ might sound something like, "What I do?" or "How I build?" So to avoid sounding like cave people, we add another word or two, such as "can" or "will" and "now" or "today," and end up with excellent-sounding questions like "What can I do right now?" and "How will I make a difference today?"

If we don't ask what we can do or make or achieve or build, then we won't do or make or achieve or build. It's just that simple. Only through action is anything accomplished.

The practice of personal accountability: We discipline our thoughts. We ask better questions. We take *action*.

· Chapter Twenty-nine ·

The Risk of Doing Nothing

A senior leader of a financial institution told me, "Sometimes people say to me, 'I don't want to take risks.' I tell them, 'You and I had better take risks, because there are about a dozen people at their computers right now in this building trying to eliminate our jobs!'" What was he really saying? None of us has guaranteed job security, and our lack of initiative today may guarantee our lack of employment tomorrow. Taking action may seem risky, but doing *nothing* is a bigger risk!

Even though there are risks involved in taking action, the alternative, inaction, is almost never the better choice:

- Action, even when it leads to mistakes, brings learning and growth. Inaction brings stagnation and atrophy.

- Action leads us toward solutions. Inaction at best does nothing and holds us in the past.

- Action requires courage. Inaction often indicates fear.

- Action builds confidence; inaction, doubt.

A friend said, "It's better to be one who is told to wait than one who waits to be told."

Decide what to do. Then take action.

CHAPTER THIRTY

"Thanks for Shopping at the Home Depot!"

One morning a few weeks into Judy's new job as a cashier at Home Depot, a young man came through her line, obviously in a hurry. He quickly plunked down a few items and a hundred-dollar bill, but the total came to only two dollars and eighty-nine cents. "Do you have anything smaller?" Judy asked. "No, I'm sorry, I don't," he said. At that moment, Judy had a choice to make.

Since she'd just opened up for the day, she had only forty dollars in her drawer. Standard procedure said that to break the hundred, she'd need to put it in a pneumatic tube and send it up to the office. But Judy thought that would take more time than her customer seemed to have—not to mention the other customers in line behind him.

So here's what she did: She handed the young man back his bill, reached down for her purse, took out the two-eighty-nine, put it in the register and tore off the receipt. She turned to her customer with a smile and said, "Thanks for shopping at the Home Depot!"

The man stood there a few moments before he figured out what she'd done. Finally, somewhat stunned, he thanked her several times and took off. As far as Judy was concerned, that was the end of it.

Two days later, her supervisor, looking both confused and amused, approached her holding an envelope.

"Judy, I need to get this straight," he said. "Did you actually buy the merchandise for one of our customers the other day?"

She had to think. "Yes, I guess I did."

"Well, he's sent you a tip," he said, "and as a Home Depot employee, I'm sure you know that you can't accept tips."

"I don't want a tip," she said, then abruptly added, "How much?"

"He wrote you a check for fifty dollars."

"Wow! How about if I endorse it and put it in the pizza fund so we can all share it?" she asked.

"OK," he said. "We can do that."

So the money went into the pizza fund, and no one thought any more of it.

The next day, though, the young man showed up in her line again. This time, he had with him his father, Bob Johnson Sr., owner of Johnson Construction Company. Question: What do contractors need? Answer: Stuff! And the better answer from Judy's perspective: stuff from the Home Depot.

The elder Mr. Johnson said to Judy, "I want

you to know that because of what you did to serve my son the other day, we've decided to start getting everything we need from you folks!"

Isn't that something? Never let it be said one person can't have an impact, especially if he or she is willing to take risks. Remember, Judy was in kind of a tight spot. The young man was in a hurry, people were lined up behind him, and standard procedure said she'd have to make them all wait while she got change. But she didn't get stressed out, thinking, "Why is this happening to me?" or just say, "Sorry, it's our policy," and make them wait. She kept her cool and decided to take action and serve her customer. That's QBQ service, and it's worth the risk.

But the story's not quite over yet. Right after the elder Mr. Johnson spoke, the younger leaned over the counter and whispered to Judy,

"Judy, I've got to know."

"You've got to know what?" she whispered back.

"The day you bought my merchandise . . . how much *higher* would you have gone?!"

CHAPTER THIRTY-ONE

Leaders at All Levels

Are you a leader? Many people wrestle with this question. "Am I a leader, or is my manager the leader? Is the company president the leader? The vice president of my division?" Or they think, "Maybe the leader is my peer who was granted the title of 'Team Leader.'"

I met one man, though, who had no question about it at all. I had just asked a group, "Are you a leader?" when he jumped up in the back row and yelled, "I'm a leader, John. You bet—I am a leader!"

I asked him, "What's your name, sir?" and he said, "Jim Leader." True story. Jim Leader. I checked his license to be sure. James D. Leader, thirty-three years old. You know what that means? For at least thirty-one years now he's been able to say confidently not only, "I'm a leader" but also, "I'm a *born* Leader!"

For most of us though, it's not that simple. Too often, we think leadership is about title, position, the number of people or dollars we manage, or tenure. I find the tenure thing especially funny. When I hear someone say boastfully, "I've been here over a dozen years!" I can just imagine someone else in that organization saying, "Yeah, and that may be your problem!"

Don't get me wrong, loyalty is an admirable quality. But the number of years one has been around does not automatically equate with being a good leader, any more than does merely having the title of manager or vice president. And certainly the things we acquire—fine cars, nice homes—are not measures of our leadership ability.

Leadership, more than anything else, is about

the way we think. It's a moment-to-moment disciplining of our thoughts. It's about practicing personal accountability and choosing to make a positive contribution, no matter what our role or "level." A receptionist, an engineer, a sales-person, a temp worker, a cashier: They all can be leaders. Judy certainly was. Parents? Absolutely. Parenting may be the most important leadership role there is. Are you a friend, Little League coach, volunteer, someone who has influence with others at work? The same principle holds true: If we think like leaders, we are leaders.

So I'll ask you again. Are you a leader? Think about it.

CHAPTER THIRTY-TWO

The Cornerstone of Leadership

Do you remember Jacob Miller from Chapter One? He was our QBQ hero from the Rock Bottom restaurant who sent his manager to get me a Diet Coke. Well, Jacob was not the only hero in that story. His manager was one, too. And it's time we gave her some recognition.

Think about this: Jacob ran to her and said, "Hey, would you get this guy a Diet Coke?" What did she say? "Yes!" But more important, what *didn't* she say? She didn't come back with one of these responses:

> "Wait a minute, Jake, who works for whom here anyway?"

"Well, I don't know, what have you done for me lately?"

"Remember when you dropped the ball?"

"If I do this for you, what will you do for me?"

Or how about this one: "Let me check your performance review and see if you're hitting your numbers. If you are, I may just help you."

She could have asked questions like these, but she didn't. Instead, in the moment, she served Jacob as she would any customer—internal or external. She didn't say, "You succeed, then I'll serve you," but rather, "I will serve you so you can succeed."

Not, "I'm the boss, so you're here for me," but, "As a leader, I'm here to help *you* reach *your* goals." "Servant leadership" is the QBQ way, and it requires a humble spirit combined with a servant's heart.

Humility is the cornerstone of leadership.

CHAPTER THIRTY-THREE

Leaders Are Not Problem Solvers

After giving a talk in my home city of Denver, I rode down the hotel elevator with a woman who had attended the session. She studiously reviewed her notes, lost in thought. Before we reached the lobby she looked up at me and spoke: "So what you're saying, John, is I should go back to the office and do other people's work for them?"

"Whoa, where did that come from?" I thought. "I must not have been clear enough about that." Let me be clear now: The QBQ is *not* about covering for people, taking on their duties and responsibilities, or doing it "all by myself." That is not a service to others, it is a disservice to everyone.

When managers step in and close the sale, when project leaders carry the team's ball, when parents clean the child's room—it teaches nothing positive and adds no real value. As my mentor, W. Steven Brown, always taught, "Leaders are not problem solvers but problem givers." They let others tackle the problem, design their own solutions, and take action. How else can people learn? How else can leaders serve?

CHAPTER THIRTY-FOUR

A Great List of Lousy Questions

Jim Ryan, president of Carlson Marketing Group, sat behind the desk. He was polite but crunched for time. He had thirty minutes.

After a few introductory remarks, the visitor—younger, without an impressive title and a bit nervous, but still hoping to capture his potential client's interest—asked, "Jim, have you ever heard questions like these?" and shared several questions he called "IQs." Then came what's commonly known in sales as a "death pause": A person asks a question and instead of an immediate response gets back an empty stare, sometimes even a glare.

The death pause hung in the room like a

heavy, foreboding cloud. The visitor was starting to sweat. An eternity later, Jim smiled and said, "Wow, that's a great list of really lousy questions!"

Yes! The IQs worked. His interest was piqued. And the questions worked because, like most people, he'd heard them before. From the guest chair I smiled back, confident a successful relationship had begun.

Now let's look at our own list of lousy questions. Each of us plays many different roles in our lives, and each of those roles has its own particular challenges and frustrations. As we read the following list of roles with IQs and QBQs, let's think about what IQs *we* might be asking, and more important, what QBQs we could use instead.

Customer service:
"When will shipping start getting orders out on time?"
"Why does the customer expect so much?"

"When will the field do it right the first time?"

"Why don't customers follow the instructions?"

QBQ: "How can I serve them?"

Sales:

"Why are our prices so high?"

"When are we going to be more competitive?"

"Why won't the customer call me back?"

"When will marketing give us better brochures?"

"Why can't manufacturing make what we sell?"

QBQs: "What can I do today to be more effective?"
"How can I add value for my customers?"

Operations or manufacturing:

"Why can't the salespeople stay within our capabilities?"

"When will they learn to sell the right specs?"

QBQ: "How can I better understand the challenges in the field?"

Management:

"Why doesn't the younger generation want to work?"

"When am I going to find good people?"

"Why aren't they motivated?"

"Who made the mistake?"

"Why can't people come in on time?"

QBQs: "How can I be a more effective coach?"

"What can I do to better understand each person on the team?"

Executive:

"Who dropped the ball?"

"When are they going to catch the vision?"

"Who will care as much as I do?"

"When will the market turn around?"

QBQs: "How can I be a better leader?"
"What can I do to show I care?"
"How can I communicate better?"

The "Front Line":

"Why do we have to go through all
this change?"

"When is someone going to train me?"

"Why don't I get paid more?"

"Who's going to clarify my job?"

"When is management going to get their
act together?"

"Who's going to give us the vision?"

QBQs: "What can I do to be more
productive?"

"How can I adapt to the changing
environment?"
"What can I do to develop myself?"

Marketing:
"When will the salespeople deliver our
programs?"
"Why won't the field learn more about
our new products?"

**QBQs: "What can I do to understand the
sales reps' frustrations?"
"How can I learn more about
what the customer needs?"**

And from the world outside of work . . .

Parent:
"When is my child going to listen to me?"
"Why does she hang out with those
kids?"
"When will he open up?"

"Who made the mess in here?"

"Why can't you be more like your sister?"

QBQs: "How can I get to know him better?"

"What can I do to improve my parenting skills?"

"How can I simply help her get through these tough years?"

Teenager:

"When are my parents going to get it?"

"Why don't they like my friends?"

"Why is my teacher so mean and unfair?"

QBQs: "How can I show more respect to Mom and Dad?"

"What can I do to communicate more effectively?"

"How can I improve my study habits?"

Spouse/Partner:
"Why doesn't he let go of that old issue?"
"When will she appreciate me more?"
"Why don't you start exercising?"

**QBQs: "How can I improve myself
          today?"
      "What can I do to help her out?"**

Neighbor:
"Why are they so unfriendly?"

QBQ: "How can I be a better friend?"

Volunteer:
"Why do I have to do everything myself?"

**QBQ: "What can I do to set better
        boundaries and just say 'no'?"**

IQs or QBQs? The choice is up to us. Let's choose wisely, because the questions we ask can make all the difference in the world.

CHAPTER THIRTY-FIVE

The Spirit of the QBQ

There's a well-established legal principle that says there's a difference between the "letter" and the "spirit" of the law. The letter of the law refers to the specific words used in the law itself. The spirit refers to the underlying concepts and intentions behind the law. The general idea is that compliance with the letter of the law should be in alignment with the spirit of the law.

Using the same concept in our case, the letter of the QBQ would be the guidelines:

1. Begin with "What" or "How," (**not** "Why," "When," or "Who").

2. Contain an "I" (**not** "they," "them," "we," or "you").
3. Focus on action.

The *spirit* of the QBQ is personal accountability:

- No more victim thinking, procrastinating, or blaming.
- I can only change me.
- Take action!

I mention this because it's possible to construct a question that follows the letter of the QBQ but conflicts with the spirit. Consider these:

"What can I do to *make you change?*"
"How can I *avoid responsibility* in this matter?"

"What action can I take right now to *do the wrong thing?*"
Or my son's favorite, "Who can I *blame today?*"

OK, my son's doesn't even follow the letter. The others do, yet they're clearly not QBQs. The principle is this: If a question conflicts with the spirit of the QBQ, it isn't a QBQ.

Playing with QBQs like these can be fun. But when the time comes to construct a meaningful question, remember that the only questions that will help us practice personal accountability are those that follow both the letter *and* the spirit of the QBQ.

Wisdom

Wisdom: what we learn after we know it all.

I'm not a finished product. Are you?

We Buy Too Many Books

We attend too many seminars. We take too many classes. We buy too many books. We play too many audios in our cars. It's all wasted if we're unclear on what learning really is: Learning is not attending, listening, or reading. Nor is it merely gaining knowledge. Learning is really about translating *knowing* what to do into *doing* what we know. It's about changing.

If we have not changed we have not learned. What have you learned today?

· CHAPTER THIRTY-EIGHT ·

A Final Picture

The Miller family was driving down the highway on a windy Sunday afternoon when we came upon the most amazing scene: In a field off to the side of the road, we saw a man dive from his wheelchair into a sea of newspapers that were blowing around in the Denver wind. He was trying to catch them, but the wind was strong, and in a moment the field was almost completely covered. From the back of the van, Kristin, our oldest, yelled, "Dad, let's go help that guy!" So we quickly parked, and all of us raced out to help. As we chased down papers, hugging them to our chests, I wondered what had happened.

"Many hands make light work," the saying

goes, and the job was soon done. As we gathered around the gentleman, he rested on one hip, clutched the few papers he had been able to nab, and silently searched for words.

One of the kids asked him, "What happened?" and after struggling back into his wheelchair, with one arm shaking almost to the point of uselessness, he said, "I got home and noticed a whole bundle had disappeared from my pickup. Driving back this direction, I saw the field covered and I couldn't believe my eyes!"

Without really thinking it through first, I asked, "And you were going to pick them up all by yourself?"

He looked at me as if I didn't get it and said, "I couldn't just leave them. *It was my mess.*"

My mess. My responsibility. What a powerful picture of personal accountability. As we've said throughout this book, personal accountability is not blaming, complaining, and putting things off, but instead asking questions like "What can

I do?" and taking action. We've offered guidelines for constructing better questions—all QBQs begin with "What" or "How," contain an "I," and focus on action—suggesting that asking QBQs is the way to start disciplining our thoughts and making better choices.

As we go out now and apply the QBQ in our own lives, let's always remember the real reason we're doing it. We're doing it so we can be more like the people we've read about in this book: Jacob, the server at the Rock Bottom restaurant; Stacey's father, the pilot; Bonita, the flight attendant; Judy, the cashier at the Home Depot; and our "handicapped" friend with the newspapers (his name was Brian), who got down and crawled around in a field because it was "his mess."

None of these people knew about the QBQ, but each embodied its spirit. The rest of us, though, with me standing at the front of the line, need the QBQ. We may not need it every minute of every day, but we need it often enough for it to make a real difference in our lives.

We need the QBQ so our organizations can be places where, instead of finger-pointing, procrastinating, and "we-they"ing ourselves into the ground, we bring out the best in each other, work together the way teams are supposed to, and make great things happen.

It's an exciting vision that I hope speaks as loudly to you as it does to me, because if more people practiced personal accountability, the world would be a far better place.

The QBQ. The Question Behind the Question. May it serve you well in all you do.

CHAPTER THIRTY-NINE

The Motor of Learning

Repetition is the motor of learning.
  What's that again?
Repetition is the motor of learning.
  I beg your pardon?
Repetition is . . .
  OK, I get it!
Great. So now that you've finished the book, read it again.

At www.QBQ.com you can learn more about what *QBQ!* can do for you and your organization!

- **Explore the QBQ! training system.** *QBQ! Achieving Excellence by Practicing Personal Accountability* goes beyond the book, enabling your *organization* to eliminate blame, complaining, and procrastination by making personal accountability a core value. This exciting, multimedia tool is practical, user-friendly, and designed to be implemented by your in-house facilitators. Imagine the difference when personal accountability is a permanent part of your organizational culture and a way of life for your people. The *QBQ!* training system can make it happen!

- **Have the author of *QBQ!* speak to your group.** There's nothing like a live event to inspire passion and excitement for personal accountability. Experience the energy, humor, and power of John G. Miller's dynamic keynote presentation.

- **Join the *QBQ!* community**. Learn more about *QBQ!*, its life-changing impact, and how you can help spread the message of personal accountability.

QBQ, Inc.
Helping Organizations Make Personal Accountability a Core Value
Denver, CO
(800) 774-0737
(303) 286-9900
e-mail: staff@QBQ.com
www.QBQ.com

Thanks to each of
you for laughing and
learning with me!
The QBQ works —
enjoy!

John G. Miller

QBQ!

Share It with Others

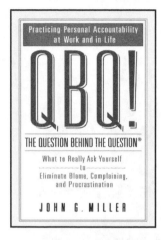

A powerful tool to help businesses, organizations, and families make personal accountability a core value.

Penguin Group (USA) Inc. books are available at special quantity discounts for bulk purchases for sales promotions, premiums, fund-raising, or educational use. Customized books or book excerpts can be created to fit specific needs.

To order bulk copies for give-aways, premiums, distribution to employees, sales promotions, or education, contact:

> **Penguin Group Premium Sales**
> phone: 212-366-2612
> fax: 212-366-2679
> www.penguin.com/corporatesales

For fund-raising or non-bookstore reselling, contact:

> **Penguin Group Special Markets**
> phone: 212-366-2612
> fax: 212-366-2679

To order individual copies, contact:

> **Penguin Group Consumer Sales**
> phone: 800-788-6262
> fax: 201-256-0017